TIME
FOR KIDS

X WHY Z
SPACE

By Mark Shulman and James Buckley Jr.

TIME FOR KIDS
Managing Editor, TIME FOR KIDS Magazine: Nellie Gonzalez Cutler
Creative Director: Jennifer Kraemer-Smith
Project Editor: Vickie An

TIME HOME ENTERTAINMENT
Publisher Jim Childs
Vice President and Associate Publisher Margot Schupf
Vice President, Finance Vandana Patel
Executive Director, Marketing Services Carol Pittard
Executive Director, Business Development Suzanne Albert
Executive Director, Marketing Susan Hettleman
Associate Publishing Director Megan Pearlman
Associate Director of Publicity Courtney Greenhalgh
Assistant General Counsel Simone Procas
Assistant Director, Special Sales Ilene Schreider
Senior Financial Analyst John Champlin
Senior Marketing Manager, Sales Marketing Danielle Costa
Senior Marketing Manager, Children's Category Amanda Lipnick
Associate Production Manager Amy Mangus
Associate Prepress Manager Alex Voznesenskiy
Associate Project Manager Stephanie Braga

Editorial Director Stephen Koepp
Senior Editor Roe D'Angelo
Managing Editor Matt DeMazza
Copy Chief Rina Bander
Design Manager Anne-Michelle Gallero
Editor, Children's Books Jonathan White
Assistant Managing Editor Gina Scauzillo
Editorial Assistant Courtney Mifsud

Created at Oomf, Inc.
www.Oomf.com

By Mark Shulman and James Buckley Jr.
Designed by Bill Madrid
Educational Consultant: Kara Pranikoff

Special thanks: Keith Aurelio, Katherine Barnet, Brad Beatson, Jeremy Biloon, Susan Chodakiewicz, Lena Cigleris, Rose Cirrincione, Felton Davis, Assu Etsubneh, Mariana Evans, Christine Font, Alison Foster, Charlie Gomez, Hillary Hirsch, David Kahn, Jean Kennedy, Kimberly Marshall, Nina Mistry, Dave Rozzelle, Matthew Ryan, Ricardo Santiago, Divyam Shrivastava, Adriana Tierno

For information on TIME FOR KIDS magazine for the
classroom or home, go to TIMEFORKIDS.COM
or call 1-800-777-8600.
For subscriptions to SI KIDS, go to
SIKIDS.COM or call 1-800-889-6007.

Published by TIME FOR KIDS Books,
An imprint of Time Home Entertainment Inc.
1271 Avenue of the Americas, 6th floor
New York, NY 10020

ISBN 10: 1-61893-126-1
ISBN 13: 978-1-61893-126-9
Library of Congress Control Number: 2014946436

TIME FOR KIDS is a trademark of Time Inc.

We welcome your comments and suggestions about TIME FOR KIDS Books. Please write to us at:
TIME FOR KIDS Books, Attention: Book Editors, P.O. Box 11016, Des Moines, IA 50336-1016
If you would like to order any of our hardcover Collector's Edition books, please call us at 1-800-327-6388 (Monday through Friday, 7 a.m. to 8 p.m., or Saturday, 7 a.m. to 6 p.m., Central Time).
1 QGT 14

X WHY Z SPACE

CONTENTS

WELCOME!

WHY IS SPACE SO AMAZING?

Kids love to explore. It's no wonder they have questions about everything in the world, and everything beyond the world too.

Whether it's about the farthest star or the closest rock, each chapter in this book will give you the answer.

Remember to look for the  boxes to find out even more.

It's out of this world!

WHY IS SPACE SO BIG?

Space is big because it is infinite (*in*-fin-it). That means it is a never-ending place. The reason space doesn't end is because it is always getting bigger. It's like counting with numbers. No matter how far you go, you can always go farther.

THE BIG BANG

WHY IS THE START OF THE UNIVERSE CALLED THE BIG BANG?

Most scientists think the entire universe began about 14 billion years ago. At the time, every single thing in the universe was packed tightly together. Then, suddenly, there was a hot burst of energy! This "big bang" scattered everything in every direction. After a while, it grew into the universe we know today. And it's still expanding!

OUR SUN

The sun's rays are filled with energy.
Its heat and light make life on Earth possible.

WHY IS THE SUN CALLED A STAR?

Because it is a star! Our sun is just the closest star to Earth. This is why it looks so much larger than the other stars we see. If you were standing on a planet trillions of miles away, our sun would look like all the other twinkling dots in the night sky.

WHY DO WE NEED THE SUN?

We need the sun for many reasons. The sun's heat keeps us warm. Its light lets us see. Energy from the sun helps plants to grow. Plants give us oxygen to breathe. They are also a source of food for many animals. Without the sun, there would be no life on Earth. The planet would be a frozen, dark and empty place.

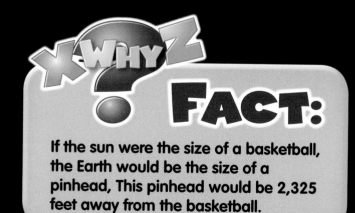

X-WHY-Z FACT:

If the sun were the size of a basketball, the Earth would be the size of a pinhead, This pinhead would be 2,325 feet away from the basketball.

Earth

Why Does the Sun Have Spots?

Sunspots are dark blobs on the sun's surface. The patches appear in places that are cooler than the rest of the sun. But these spots are definitely not cold. They can be as hot as 8,000 degrees! Sunspots last a short time. As they heat up again, the spots disappear.

WHY DOES THE SUN RISE AND SET?

No matter what it looks like, the sun is not moving. The Earth is! Our planet is always spinning. It takes one day for the Earth to make a full spin. When the sun "rises" in the morning, your part of the world is facing the sun. When the sun "sets" at night, your part of the world is turning away from the sun. Nighttime for you is daytime in another part of the globe.

WHY DOES SUNLIGHT TAKE SO LONG TO REACH EARTH?

Light from the sun takes about eight minutes to reach the Earth. That's because the sun is 93 million miles away. So the sunset you see really happened eight minutes earlier!

OUR SOLAR SYSTEM

Earth is one of eight planets that circle the Sun.
This group of planets is our Solar System.

Mercury

Venus

Earth

Mars

Jupiter

WHY DO PLANETS CIRCLE THE SUN?

Gravity is the force that keeps everything in our solar system circling the sun. Gravity works like a magnet. The bigger the magnet, the stronger the tug. The sun is the largest and heaviest object in the solar system. It has more gravity than anything else. The motion of the planets works against the sun's pull. It keeps them from crashing into the sun!

Saturn

Uranus

Neptune

WHY IS OUR STAR SYSTEM CALLED THE "SOLAR SYSTEM"?

Our sun is a star called Sol. Together, the planets and other objects that move around a star are known as a system. Our solar system is named after the star at the center of it all.

WHY ARE PLANETS ROUND?

Planets and stars are round for the same reason. They are always being pulled by gravity. Think of gravity as a giant fist. This fist is always squeezing against stars and planets. And what happens when something is squeezed with the same force in every direction? It ends up shaped like a ball!

WHY IS MERCURY SO HOT?

Mercury is the closest planet to the sun. This makes it a very hot place. Not all of Mercury is hot, though. It does not spin in the same way Earth does. It turns much slower. Mercury takes 59 Earth days to spin once around. So one side of the planet faces the sun for a long time. The other side is dark and cold.

X-WHY-Z FACT:

Mercury is named for the winged messenger of the ancient Roman gods. The Greeks called him Hermes.

WHY IS MERCURY SO HARD TO SEE IN THE NIGHT SKY?

Mercury is the smallest planet. Since it is so close to the sun, it can get lost in the sun's glare. But it's not impossible to spot. You just have to know when to look. Mercury is best seen before sunrise or after sunset. It looks like a tiny glowing speck in the sky, much like a star. So how could ancient astronomers tell it was a planet? Because it moves!

PLANET FACT:

1 Mercury year = 88 Earth days
3 Mercurys nearly equals 1 Earth
0 Moons, 0 Rings

WHY CAN'T WE SEE THE SURFACE OF VENUS?

The surface of Venus is shaded by thick clouds. This heavy fog covers the entire planet. It is made up of poison gases. Light does not go very far through these gases. Even telescopes that can see great distances cannot see through the clouds.

PLANET FACT:

1 Venus year = 225 Earth days
1 Venus nearly equals 1 Earth
0 Moons, 0 Rings

WHY IS VENUS THE HOTTEST PLANET IN THE SOLAR SYSTEM?

It's true that Mercury is closer to the sun. But Venus is hotter. Heat from the sun goes through the thick clouds that surround Venus. Those clouds trap the heat. Under the clouds, Venus's temperature can rise higher than 900 degrees. This picture shows the hottest spots in purple.

WHYZ FACT:

Venus is named for the Roman goddess of love. It is the only planet named for a woman. The Greek name for Venus is Aphrodite (aff-row-*die*-tee).

WHY IS MARS RED?

Mars is covered by a layer of rust. Huge wind storms on Mars often swirl the rusty red dust all over the planet. That's why Mars looks red from here on Earth.

X-WHY-Z FACT:

Mars is named for the Roman god of war. His Greek name is Ares.

WHY ARE MARTIANS OUR FAVORITE ALIENS?

Nearby Mars can be seen more easily from Earth than any other planet. Scientists have not found life on Mars yet. But there are clues that water used to flow on the planet. And if there was water, was there life once too? It makes sense that people might wonder if there are beings living "next door." Many science fiction books and movies feature Martians. So our fascination only grows!

PLANET FACT:

1 Mars year = 686 Earth days
1 Mars nearly equals one-half Earth
2 Moons, 0 Rings

WHY DOES NASA SEND ROBOTS TO MARS?

We can learn a lot about our own planet by studying the ones closest to us. But it can take months to reach Mars or Venus. Also, the environments (en-*vie*-run-ments) on those planets are very harsh. Humans can't survive there. That's why we build robots to help us explore those lands.

WHY DID CURIOSITY NEED JETS TO LAND?

The Mars *Curiosity* rover needed to land softly to keep its parts working. So NASA built a special spacecraft to help. It had jets at each corner. The jets let the craft hover above the ground. Then the craft used wires to slowly lower the rover down. *Curiosity* landed safe and sound!

X-WHY-Z FACT:

In 1967, *Mariner 4* took the first photos of Mars from orbit. In 1971, the *Mars 2* lander became the first man-made object to land on Mars.

WHY IS JUPITER CALLED A "GAS GIANT"?

Jupiter is not solid like Earth or Mars. It is made almost completely of gas. Jupiter, Saturn, Uranus and Neptune are all known as gas giants because of their large size. But Jupiter is the biggest by far.

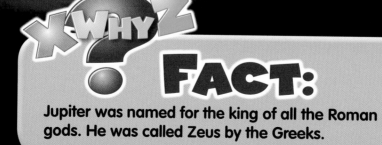

X-WHY Z FACT:

Jupiter was named for the king of all the Roman gods. He was called Zeus by the Greeks.

WHY ARE THINGS HEAVIER ON JUPITER?

Jupiter is the largest planet. It has the most powerful gravity. The strong pull of its gravity makes everything weigh more. Say you weigh 75 pounds on Earth. On Jupiter, you'd weigh more than 175 pounds! Can you lift 175 pounds? If not, you wouldn't be able to stand up on Jupiter.

Earth

Jupiter

PLANET FACT:
1 Jupiter year = 12 Earth years
1 Jupiter nearly equals 11 Earths
63 moons, 4 rings

WHY DOES SATURN HAVE RINGS?

Saturn is famous for its dazzling rings. The colorful bands circle the planet because of Saturn's strong gravity. The rings are made up of billions of parts. They range in size from tiny ice crystals to larger moons. Saturn's rings are very wide. They can fit easily between the Earth and our moon. The rings are thin, though. They are only about 30 feet thick.

1 Saturn year = 30 Earth years
1 Saturn nearly equals 9 Earths
31 moons, more than 1,000 rings

PLANET FACT:

WHY IS TITAN DIFFERENT FROM ALL OTHER MOONS?

The solar system has dozens upon dozens of moons. But Saturn's moon Titan is the only one with a thick atmosphere (*at*-muss-feer). An atmosphere is the bubble of air or gas around a planet. Earth's atmosphere makes life possible. Scientists wonder if life might be brewing under Titan's bubble too.

X-WHY-Z FACT:

Saturn is named for the Roman god who watched over farms and farmers. He was also the god of time. His Greek name was Cronos. He was Zeus/Jupiter's father.

WHY DOES URANUS SPIN DIFFERENTLY?

Almost every planet in our solar system spins the way Earth spins. One pole is close to the top. The other pole is close to the bottom. Uranus is different. It spins with its poles on the side, like a bead on a necklace. Some scientists think Uranus was struck by many large objects early on. These crashes would have caused the planet's odd tilt.

WHY DOES URANUS LOOK BLUE?

Uranus is one of the four gas giants. One of the gases surrounding the planet is methane (*meth*-ayne). When sun shines on methane, the gas has a blue-green color.

PLANET FACT:

1 Uranus year = 84 Earth years
1 Uranus nearly equals 4 Earths
27 moons, 11 rings

FACT:

Uranus is named for the Roman god of the heavens. The Romans changed the names of many of the Greek gods, but Uranus kept his Greek name.

WHY DID IT TAKE SO LONG TO FIND URANUS?

Up until the late 18th century, people thought there were six planets. That's because Saturn is the furthest planet you can spot with the naked eye. It wasn't until 1781 that William Herschel discovered Uranus. He had the help of a strong telescope.

WHY IS THE WIND ON NEPTUNE SO FAST?

Neptune has the fastest winds in the solar system. This is because the planet spins so quickly. The wind on faraway Neptune can go above 1,300 miles per hour. That is much stronger than the fastest winds on Earth, which almost never go higher than 200 miles per hour.

PLANET FACT:

1 Neptune year = 165 Earth years
1 Uranus nearly equals 4 Earths
13 moons, 4 rings

WHY DOES NEPTUNE'S MOON TRITON STAND OUT?

Triton is the only large moon in the solar system that circles its planet backwards! Triton is also one of the coldest places in our solar system. The temperature is about –400 degrees. Why is it so chilly? The moon is almost 3 billion miles from the sun. It gets very little heat and sunlight. But even if it did, Triton's icy surface would reflect a lot of the light.

X-WHY-Z ? FACT:

Neptune is named for the Roman god of the oceans. His Greek name is Poseidon.

WHY ISN'T PLUTO CALLED A PLANET ANY MO[RE]

Pluto is now called a dwarf planet. In 2006, scientists changed the rules for planets. Dwarf planets are smaller than regular plan[ets]. They are even smaller than Earth's moon. Dwarf planets, like Pluto, are also very far from the sun. Because of this, they are par[t] made of ice. So far, there are six known dwarf planets in our sola[r]. But it's possible there are many more.

X-WHYZ FACT:

Eleven-year-old Venetia Burney gave Pluto its name in 1930. The planet is named for the Roman god of the underworld. Pluto's Greek name is Hades.

WHY ARE SOME PLANETS CALLED "EXOPLANETS"?

"Exo-" means "outside" in Greek. Exoplanets are planets that are outside of our solar system. These planets orbit other stars. Scientists have found many, many exoplanets. Some are the size of Earth. In our solar system, Earth is the only planet we know of that supports life. But that doesn't mean planets in other systems can't!

PLANET FACT:

1 Pluto year = 246 Earth years
More than 5 Plutos equals 1 Earth
5 moons, ? rings (it's too far to tell!)

OUR PLANET

We live on Planet Earth.

It is just the right temperature for life to grow.

WHY IS EARTH THE ONLY PLANET WITH LIFE?

The answer is all around us!
Earth is covered by a layer of
air called the atmosphere. Air
lets people, animals, and plants
breathe. It protects us from the
sun's powerful rays. Air also keeps
our planet the right temperatures. Plus,
Earth is the only planet with lots of water.
We need water to survive. These things
make life on Earth possible.

WHY DO WE SPLIT EARTH INTO HEMISPHERES?

Hemi- means "half." Sphere (*sfeer*) is the name for the shape of a ball. A hemisphere (*hem*-ih-sfeer) is half of a ball. Earth is divided into four main parts. They are the northern, southern, eastern and western hemispheres. This makes our planet easier to study.

Equator
Longitude
Latitude

X WHY Z ? FACT:

Mapmakers draw make-believe lines on maps to help measure distances. The lines make it easier for us to find places. Latitude (*lat*-ih-tood) lines run east to west. Longitude (*lonj*-ih-tood) lines run north to south.

WHY DOES THE EQUATOR GO AROUND EARTH?

The equator (ee-*kway*-ter) is an imaginary line on our globe. This line runs all around the center of the Earth. It is found exactly between the North and South Poles. It splits the Earth into the northern and southern hemispheres. The equator is always the closest part of the planet to the sun. That's why the places near the equator are hotter than others.

WHY DOES EARTH HAVE DAYS AND NIGHTS?

Day and night happen because Earth spins. When places on Earth face the sun, it is daytime. When places on Earth face away from the sun, it is night. That means when you are eating your lunch at noon, it's midnight on the other side of the globe.

X-WHY-Z FACT:

In summer, the North Pole tilts toward the sun. During this time, the sun does not set in those places. It is light outside 24 hours a day. They call this the "Midnight Sun."

South Pole

North Pole

WHY DOES EARTH SPIN?

Our solar system began as a swirling cloud of dust and gas. About 5 billion years ago, the cloud started to collapse. This caused everything inside to spin faster and faster. Over time, the sun formed at the center. The dust and gas clumped together to form planets. And everything was still spinning! When objects move in space, they don't stop unless an outside force stops them. Nothing has stopped Earth from its original spin.

WHY IS AN EARTH DAY 24 HOURS LONG?

A day is the time it takes a planet to make one full rotation (row-*tay*-shun), or spin. People have been splitting the day into 24 equal parts since ancient times. We call these parts "hours." It takes Earth 24 hours to spin once on its axis.

WHY IS A YEAR 365 DAYS LONG?

A year is the time it takes for Earth to make one trip around the sun. As the Earth moves around the sun it is also spinning. One rotation of the Earth is the same as one day. The Earth spins around 365 times by the time it moves once around the sun. That's why there are 365 days in a year.

Fall

WHY DO WE HAVE LEAP YEARS?

A year is really 365 days and six hours long. After four years, each year's extra six hours add up to a full day. So every four years, we add an extra day to our calendar. That day is February 29.

Summer

WHY DOES EARTH HAVE SEASONS?

Earth's poles don't point straight up and down. They tilt a bit. This tilt gives the Earth its seasons. Only one pole is angled toward the sun at a time. When the North Pole is tilted toward the sun, it's summer. When it's tilted away from the sun, it's winter. This is true for the South Pole too. What about spring and fall? During those seasons, the sun shines evenly on the entire planet.

Spring

FEB 29

X-WHY-Z FACT:

If you were born on February 29, you only have a birthday once every four years. So when your friends turn 100, you'll be 25!

Winter

WHY DO THE CONTINENTS LOOK LIKE PUZZLE PIECES?

Very, very long ago

Very long ago

Long ago, the Earth's continents were one giant land mass. Scientists named this Pangaea (pan-*jee*-uh). Over millions of years, Pangaea slowly started to break up. The different parts moved across the Earth's crust. Over time, they formed the continents we know today. In fact, the continents are still moving. But they move far too slowly for us to notice.

Long ago

X WHY Z

? FACT:

Only about 30% of Earth's surface is covered by land. The other 70% is covered by water.

Today

WHY DOES EARTH APPEAR BLUE AND GREEN FROM SPACE?

From space, the Earth looks like a blue ball with patches of white and green. The blue is water. Oceans cover most of the Earth. The green and brown areas are the land. And the white parts are clouds and ice. Earth is the only planet to have these colors. This is because it's the only planet with air and water.

WHY IS EARTH MADE OF LAYERS?

core

outer core

mantle

crust

The Earth is made from rocks and minerals pulled together by gravity. Scientists believe that as the Earth was forming, the hottest and heaviest rocks sank to the center. The lighter rocks moved toward the outer edges. As the pieces settled, they formed four different layers. They are the inner core, outer core, mantle and crust.

XWHYZ FACT:

A geologist (jee-*ah*-luh-jist) is a scientist who studies the Earth and its rocks and minerals.

46

WHY DO EARTHQUAKES HAPPEN?

The Earth's top layer, or crust, is made up of giant moving puzzle pieces called plates. The places where plates meet are called faults. Sometimes the plates move under or over each other. Or they push into each other. All this movement causes the Earth to shake, rattle, and roll. *Earthquake!*

WHY DO VOLCANOS ERUPT?

Deep inside the Earth is hot, melted rock called magma. Sometimes too much of it builds up. This can cause a lot of pressure. The pressure forces the magma up through the volcano's vent. It's like squeezing thick toothpaste through a narrow tube. When magma reaches the top, the volcano erupts. When it bursts out of the crater, it is red-hot lava.

X-WHY-Z FACT: The sides of a volcano are made of cool, hardened lava. You can tell a volcano has erupted many times if it is tall!

WHY IS THE CENTER OF THE EARTH SO HOT?

The center, or core, of the Earth was the first part of the planet to form. It is extremely hot. As the Earth grew larger, the newer layers of the planet trapped the heat in the middle. Today, Earth's core is almost as hot as when it was formed billions of years ago.

X WHY Z FACT:

Volcanos are named for Vulcan, the Roman god of fire who built armor in his furnace. Vulcan's Greek name is Hephaestus (huh-*fess*-tuss).

WHY ARE THERE MOUNTAINS ON EARTH?

Mountains are formed in many ways. Remember those plates in the Earth's crust? Some mountains are formed when these plates crash together. The impact causes the land to be pushed up, and a mountain forms. Other mountains are formed by volcanos over many years.

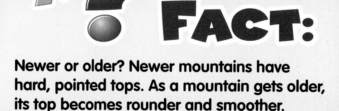

X-WHY-Z FACT:

Newer or older? Newer mountains have hard, pointed tops. As a mountain gets older, its top becomes rounder and smoother.

WHY IS THE GRAND CANYON SO BIG?

The enormous Grand Canyon is in the state of Arizona. Over millions of years, the Colorado River slowly carved away layer after layer of the desert floor until a deep valley formed. This process is called erosion (ee-*row*-zhun). The Grand Canyon is one of the world's largest and most beautiful canyons.

X-WHY-Z FACT:

The Grand Canyon is the same size as the state of Delaware. The bottom of the canyon is a mile down from the top. To reach the bottom, many people ride a mule down a steep trail.

WHY ARE THE POLES FROZEN?

The North and South Poles are covered in ice all year round. This is because the polar areas don't get as much heat from the sun to warm them up. The Earth's poles never move as close to the sun as the equator, where you'll find hot tropical rainforests.

X-WHY-Z FACT:

Icebergs are like giant ice cubes that broke away from larger sheets of ice. Icebergs can be as small as a truck or as high and wide as a hill.

WHY DO THE NORTHERN LIGHTS APPEAR IN THE SKY?

The Northern Lights are one of nature's most amazing sights. You can see them near the North Pole. This dazzling light show happens when charged particles from the sun slam into Earth's upper atmosphere. The crash creates a dancing show of red, green, purple and blue lights in the sky. Similar lights can be seen near the South Pole.

WHY DOES THE MOON HAVE "PHASES"?

During the month, it might seem like the moon is changing shape. It isn't. The moon is always shaped like a ball. On Earth, we only see the part of the moon that is lit by the sun. For a few days each month, we see the whole lit side. We call this phase a full moon. The rest of the month, we only see part of the lit side. When we can't see the lit part at all, this phase is called a new moon.

WHY IS A MONTH ABOUT 30 DAYS LONG?

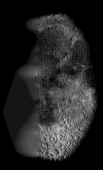

It takes the moon about 30 days to move once around the Earth. We call this length of time a month. The word month comes from the same word that means moon. The moon makes 12 trips around the Earth in one year. That's why one year is equal to 12 months.

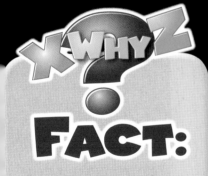

X-WHY-Z FACT:

The Earth is four times wider than the moon—but 81 times heavier!

WHY DOES THE MOON STAY SO CLOSE TO EARTH?

Earth has more powerful gravity than the moon because Earth is a lot large That gravity pulls on the moon, keeping it moving on a path, or orbit, around Earth. The moon's orbit is not a perfect circle. But the moon and Earth are always about 238,000 miles apart.

FACT:

Just like the sun rises and sets, the moon rises and sets around the same time every day. See if you can catch the moonrise tonight!

WHY IS MOONLIGHT REALLY SUNLIGHT?

The moon has no light of its own. So how can it shine so brightly at night? The moon's glow is really sunlight bouncing off the moon's surface.

WHY ARE THERE HOLES ON THE MOON?

The moon is covered in holes called craters (*kray*-ters). These craters were caused by meteors, which are large flying rocks that have smacked into the moon. Meteors that hit Earth have also left craters. But the holes are mostly covered by dirt or water.

XWHYZ? FACT:

If you can jump over a cereal box on Earth, you can jump over a car on the moon!

WHY CAN PEOPLE JUMP SO HIGH ON THE MOON?

It all comes back to gravity! The moon is a lot smaller than Earth. So the moon's gravity has less force. This lets people jump higher than normal. You would weigh much less on the moon. People who weigh 100 pounds on Earth weigh only about 16 pounds on the moon.

STARS & BEYOND

The stars you see are very, very far away. And you'll find much more than stars in the night sky.

WHY DO STARS TWINKLE IN THE SKY?

The light from other stars can shine as bright as our sun. It's even brighter if the star is bigger. But these stars are very far away. The light has to travel great distances. That's why the stars look so small in the night sky. When starlight hits our atmosphere, the air breaks up the light. This gives the star its twinkle.

WHY DO STARS FORM?

Stars begin as swirling clouds of gas and dust. Over millions of years, as gravity pulls the cloud closer together, it spins faster and gets hotter. A heavy, hot core forms in the middle. The core becomes so hot it starts to burn. That's what a star is: a giant ball of burning gas in space.

WHY DO SOME STARS SEEM BRIGHTER THAN OTHERS?

Brighter stars are usually larger and closer to Earth than other stars. The brightest star in our sky is called Sirius. It is one of the closest stars to Earth. As a star, Sirius is about twice as big as our sun, and it shines much brighter.

WHY IS EVERYTHING ON A STAR A GAS?

Why does boiling water turn to steam? Because very hot things turn to gas. That's true on a star too. Every star burns the gases hydrogen and helium at millions of degrees. Iron, copper and other metals can be found on stars. But those metals are so hot, they're not solid—they're gas.

WHY IS SPACE MEASURED IN LIGHT-YEARS?

Normally, we measure distances between places in miles. But outside our solar system, the distances are far too great. Instead, scientists use a measurement called a light-year. It's the distance that light can travel in 365 days. Believe it or not, one light-year is equal to 6,000,000,000,000 miles. That's six trillion miles a year!

WHY IS THE CLOSEST STAR SO FAR AWAY?

Our sun is a star called Sol. It is 93 million miles away from Earth. Beyond Sol, the closest star is called Proxima Centauri (sen-*tar*-ree). It is about four light-years from Earth. That means if Proxima Centauri ever stopped shining, it would take four years for us to notice.

WHY ARE STARS SO POWERFUL?

Every sun is a giant ball of super-hot gases and plasma (*plaz*-muh), a gas-like substance. A star has the power of many, many atomic bombs exploding at the same time. Inside our fiery sun, temperatures rise past 27 million degrees F. The sun is so incredibly powerful, it can give you a sunburn from 93 million miles away. Never look directly at the sun. It will harm your eyes.

X-WHY-Z FACT:

Many stars have twins. Planets that orbit twin stars have two suns.

WHY DO COMETS HAVE TAILS?

Comets are made mostly of ice. When a comet travels near a star, the star's heat boils off bits of the comet. Those melting bits form a cloud that follows the speeding comet. That's what looks like a tail.

WHY ARE METEORS CALLED SHOOTING STARS?

Meteors are pieces that have broken away from asteroids or comets. Meteors that enter our atmosphere burn up in the sky as they fall to Earth. This creates what looks like a trail of fire in the sky, or a "shooting star." A meteor that lands on Earth is called a meteorite (*mee*-tee-or-ite).

WHY ARE ASTEROIDS AND COMETS DIFFERENT?

Asteroids are hunks of metal and rock that orbit fairly close to a star. Comets are made of dust, ice and rocks. They have wide, oval orbits that can take them very far from their star.

X-WHY-Z FACT:

Nearly all of the asteroids in our solar system are found between Mars and Jupiter. This area is called the Asteroid Belt.

WHY ARE GALAXIES SO ENORMOUS?

A galaxy is a group of hundreds of billions of stars. Galaxies orbit the universe together as one big family. Scientists don't know how many galaxies exist in the universe. But they do know there are several billion of them.
That's a lot of stars!

X-WHY-Z FACT: If you had a grain of sand for every star in our galaxy, you could fill a large truck. You would have 500 billion grains of sand for 500 billion stars in the Milky Way.

Why is our galaxy called the Milky Way?

Our solar system is part of a galaxy called the Milky Way. The Milky Way looks like a pale band of white light against the night sky. Ancient Greeks thought it looked like a splash of milk. That's how our galaxy got its name.

WHY DO SAILORS STUDY CONSTELLATIONS?

Constellations can work like maps at night. If you know where the constellations are, they can point you in the right direction. Sailors have used constellations for thousands of years to help them steer their ships across an empty sea.

WHY IS THE NORTH STAR SO IMPORTANT?

The North Star always shines brightly above the North Pole. Whenever you need to find your way at night, look for the North Star. Then you'll know which way is north, even if you're going another direction.

X-WHY-Z FACT:

A constellation is a group of stars that are positioned close together in the sky. Long ago, people connected those shining dots to draw imaginary pictures. Then they told their own stories about the characters in the stars.

WHY DO CONSTELLATIONS HAVE NAMES?

Most constellations got their names long ago. Ancient stargazers drew among a family of stars to make pictures. These were usually of anir objects or ancient figures. Many of our modern constellations come Greek and Latin myths.

ORION THE HUNTER

To find the mythical Greek hunter in the sky, look first for the three bright stars that form his "belt." The rest of him will follow!

CANIS MAJO

Its name means Great Dog. Sirius, the Star, is part of this constellation. In G myth, Sirius was Orion's hunting dog the brightest star in our sky.

DRACO

...constellation is named for a dragon ...eated by the famed Greek warrior ...es. Draco can be seen in the northern ... It includes two pairs of twin stars.

BIG DIPPER

The Big Dipper looks like a cup with a handle. It's actually part of an even larger constellation called Ursa Major, or Great Bear. The Greeks thought it looked like a mama bear.

SOUTHERN CROSS

This group of stars always points toward the South Pole. Navigators in the southern hemisphere use it as a guide, just as those in the north use the North Star.

X-WHY-Z FACT:

The International Astronomy Union lists 88 "official" constellations. Ancient traditions around the world have identified many more.

WHY DO PEOPLE USE THE ZODIAC?

Do you believe that looking at the stars can show you your future? If so, you believe in astrology (ah-*straw*-luh-jee). Astrologists study the zodiac (*zoh*-dee-ack) constellations to predict people's fates. These predictions are called your horoscope (*hore*-ah-scope). For thousands of years, different cultures have believed that the stars can tell us what's to come.

WHY ARE THE STARS USED IN THE ZODIAC?

There are 12 constellations of the zodiac. Each month, a different one is seen in the sky. You were born in the time of one of these 12 constellations. That constellation is your zodiac sign. Ancient sky gazers believed the position of the stars and planets in the zodiac explained your strengths and weaknesses, as well as your fate.

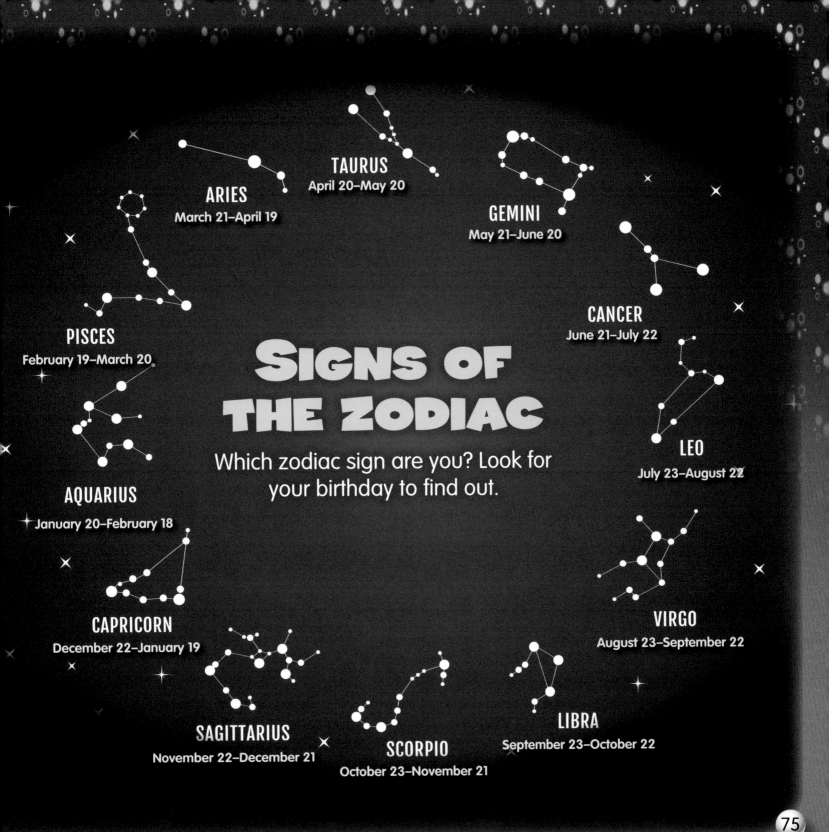

SIGNS OF THE ZODIAC

Which zodiac sign are you? Look for your birthday to find out.

ARIES
March 21–April 19

TAURUS
April 20–May 20

GEMINI
May 21–June 20

CANCER
June 21–July 22

LEO
July 23–August 22

VIRGO
August 23–September 22

LIBRA
September 23–October 22

SCORPIO
October 23–November 21

SAGITTARIUS
November 22–December 21

CAPRICORN
December 22–January 19

AQUARIUS
January 20–February 18

PISCES
February 19–March 20

SPACE EXPLORERS

What else is out in the universe?

Let's explore and find out more.

WHY IS SPACE SO DARK?

The only light in space comes from stars.
There are many billions of bright stars.
But they are very far apart.
Between the stars is darkness.

WHY IS THERE NO AIR IN SPACE?

There is air in space. It is just not collected in the same way as on Earth. All of the gases we breathe can be found everywhere in the universe. Our planet is special because of its atmosphere, which is like a bubble. It holds in oxygen and other gases that are important for life.

WHY IS IT COLD IN SPACE?

It can be both very hot and very cold in space. It just depends on if you are facing the sun. For example, the side of the space shuttle that the sun shines on can get hotter than an oven. But the side that is turned away can be colder than a freezer!

WHY CAN'T YOU HEAR SOUND IN SPACE?

Sound travels in waves through the air. Space does not have air in the same way we do on Earth. So the waves have no way to travel out there. Even if a space ship exploded, you wouldn't be able to hear it if you were in space.

WHY DO TELESCOPES MAKE STARS LOOK CLOSER?

Telescopes use lenses to make faraway objects look closer. Lenses are curved pieces of glass. If you put several lenses in a row, but spaced far apart, you can see a great distance. This is why space telescopes are so long!

WHY CAN THE HUBBLE TELESCOPE SEE OBJECTS SO FAR AWAY?

The Hubble Space Telescope is a very powerful telescope. It orbits the Earth and takes pictures of deep space. It can see farther and more clearly than any other telescope. That is because Earth's atmosphere does not get in its way. Hubble has helped change the way scientists study space.

FACT:

Large telescopes are often found on mountain tops. Up high, the fog, clouds and city lights don't block the view as much.

WHY DID SPUTNIK 1 MAKE HISTORY?

In 1957, Sputnik 1 made history as the first object launched into space to orbit the Earth. It was a meta ball about two feet wide. It made a constant beeping sound so radios could find it. Sputnik 1 was launched by the Soviet Union, which included Russia. This started a "space race" between the Soviets and the United States.

X-WHY-Z FACT:

Yuri Gagarin was the first person in space. In 1961, his rocket was launched into space for 89 minutes. No one had ever left Earth before.

TIME
THE WEEKLY NEWSMAGAZINE
MAN IN SPACE
RUSSIA'S YURI GAGARIN

WHY WERE ANIMALS SENT INTO SPACE?

At first, scientists did not know if humans could survive in space. Animals were chosen to make the journey instead. The first space traveler was a Russian dog named Laika. America's most famous animal astronaut was Ham, a chimpanzee. Ham was flown to space and back in 1961.

X WHY Z FACT:

In 1962, John Glenn was the first person to orbit the Earth. No one before had ever seen our entire planet from space.

WHY DO WE NEED ROCKETS TO REACH SPACE?

It takes a lot of energy to fight the pull of Earth's gravity. But the blast of a rocket's jets are strong enough. They lift the rocket up and away from gravity's pull, and into space. Once the rocket is in space, it needs very little power to move.

X WHY Z FACT:

The most powerful rocket ever sent into space was the Saturn V. It carried the Apollo missions toward the moon. The Saturn V was as tall as a 30-story building!

84

WHY DID ASTRONAUTS FLY IN SUCH SMALL CAPSULES?

The space capsules that carried astronauts to the moon used to be the size of a small car. This helped to save precious rocket fuel during liftoff. Space missions usually lasted only a few days. So the tiny capsule was not such a big problem for the cramped astronauts.

WHY DO ASTRONAUTS FLOAT IN SPACE?

Gravity is the force that holds stars and planets together. In space, once away from the planets, gravity gets weaker. Anything that is not tied down to something else will float away.

X-WHY-Z FACT:

Spacecraft are designed so that astronauts can breathe while traveling in space without their suits and helmets.

WHY DO ASTRONAUTS HAVE TO KEEP THEIR HELMETS ON?

The air in space is too thin for humans to survive. Temperatures can also be extremely hot or cold. Astronauts wear helmets and spacesuits for protection. The suits allow them to breathe in space.

WHY DID NEIL ARMSTRONG SAY, "THAT'S ONE SMALL STEP"?

On June 20, 1969, Apollo 11 astronaut Neil Armstrong was the first human to step onto the lunar surface. He said: "That's one small step for a man, one giant leap for mankind." Armstrong meant that the actual footstep may have been small, but people had just made a very important "leap" in human history.

X-WHY-Z

FACT:

"Eagle" was the the craft that first brought people to the moon. "The Eagle has landed" was the first radio message sent from the moon.

WHY ARE CARS STILL ON THE MOON?

Rockets were not the only vehicles that went to the moon. Lunar rovers are a kind of car that the astronauts used to travel across the lunar surface. Rovers don't have rocket engines that can lift them off the moon. It was easier to leave them behind. The next visitors can take them for a ride!

WHY WAS THE SPACE SHUTTLE BIG NEWS?

Before the space shuttle, rockets stayed in space. The astronauts' capsules were never re-used again. But the newer shuttles changed all of that. They were made to use over and over. This saved time and money for the space program. One shuttle, *Discovery*, was launched into space 39 times. That's a record!

FACT: A total of 355 different people flew on the space shuttle. This included 306 men and 49 women. They came from 16 different countries.

WHY DID THE SHUTTLE HAVE HUGE DOORS ON ITS BACK?

A job of each space shuttle was to carry satellites into space. When the huge back doors opened, a robotic arm picked up the satellite. Then it would let the satellite go floating into space. The shuttles also carried parts to help build the International Space Station.

X WHY Z FACT:

When the space shuttle landed on Earth, it would land very quickly. A parachute helped it slow down and stop. These are similar to the parachutes cars use for drag races.

SPACE EXPLORERS

WHY IS THE SPACE STATION "INTERNATIONAL"?

International means "between countries." The United States, Canada, Russia, Japan and 11 European countries built the station together. They use it as a base for space exploration.

WHY ARE THERE LONG GOLD PANELS ON THE SPACE STATION?

Huge solar panels on the International Space Station capture energy from the sun. This energy powers the space station.

GLOSSARY

asteroid hunks of metal or rock that orbit the sun

atmosphere the air that surrounds a planet

constellation a collection of stars in which people see a picture or a pattern

core the center of something, in this case the Earth

crater the giant hole in the ground caused when a meteor hits a planet or a moon

crust the outer shell of the Earth

eclipse when the Earth blocks sunlight from the moon, it's a lunar eclipse. When the moon blocks the sun, it's a solar eclipse.

erosion the process of water or wind slowly carving away a surface

exoplanet a planet far away from our own solar system

environment the place or surroundings in which a person, animal or plant lives

fault the place where two of the Earth's plates meet

galaxy a gathering of millions or billions of stars (that's a galaxy on the left)

geologist a scientist who studies the Earth, rocks, minerals and land

gravity the force that binds us to the Earth and that keeps planets orbiting the sun

hemisphere half of a sphere, or ball

light-year the distance that light travels in a year

lunar having to do with the moon

magma hot, molten, liquid rock from inside the Earth

NASA National Aeronautics and Space Administration— the part of the U.S. government that runs the space program

orbit the path that a planet or moon takes around another body in space, usually a star

rotation when an object spins like a top

solar panels devices made of special cells that capture sunlight and convert it into energy

sphere the shape of a ball

INDEX

Photo Credits (t: top, b: bottom, r: right, l: left)

Cover Images: Earth: Dreamstime.com/Tenyo Marchev; astronaut, sun, Jupiter, space shuttle: NASA.

Dollar Photo Club: 12, 14, 29b, 49t, 50(3), 70 inset, 72l

Dreamstime.com: 18b, Qju 19b, Jozsef Szasz-fabian 21b, Kuan Leong Yong 22b, PixelParticle 4, 36bkgd, Tenyo Marchev 36 main, Lukaves 42, Frenta 46t, Nigel Spiers 47, Julien Grondin 48, Tifonimages 52, Alexander Kolomietz 52b, Stephen McSweeny 53, Saiva 55, Kenneth Keifer 58, Barold 66b, Tearswept 70, 73l, Claudio Balducelli 73b, Beata Kraus 75, Mikhail Basov 81b, Rastan 82

David Gunnells (bit.ly/UeEOYR): 49b

Marie-Lan Nguyen (Wikimedia Commons): 28b

NASA: SDO 8, ESA/Hubble 10, SOHO 11b, 18, 20, 21, 22, JPL 24, 25t, 25b, 26 (2), 29tr, 30, 32, 33t, 34tl, JPL/Caltech 34, 45, 54, 56, 59, Hubble 62, Hubble 64, 65, Dan Burbank 66 main, 67b, JPL/Caltech/K. Gordon (University of Arizona) 68, G. Hüdepohl/ESO 76, 81, 82, 83, 84, 85, 86(2), 87, 88, 89, 90, 91t, 91b, 92 inset, 92 main, Caltech 95

E.M. Robins: 46b

Rufus46 (Wikimedia Commons): 33b

Shutterstock: Igor Zh. 6, Johan Swanepoel 16, Allegresse Photography 19 main, Linda Bucklin 23, MarcelClemens 26, AndInc 28, Philip Lange 31t, Yutthaphong 34b, RTImages 38, Chevanon 43b, Miha de 44, Traveller Martin 60, Yganko 72r, 73r, EpicStockmedia 77

Time Magazine: 82b, 83b

Mike Young (Wikimedia Commons): 31br